FLY FISHING

BY CLARA MacCARALD

childsworld.com

Published by The Child's World®
800-599-READ • www.childsworld.com

Photography Credits
Photographs ©: Kevin Cass/Shutterstock Images, cover, 1; SnapT Photography/Shutterstock Images, 5; Shutterstock Images, 6; Clarkand Company/iStockphoto, 9; iStockphoto, 10, 12, 13 (middle, bottom), 17; David W. Leindecker/Shutterstock Images, 13 (top); Michael Svoboda/iStockphoto, 13 (middle top, middle bottom); Rich Legg/iStockphoto, 15; J Michl/iStockphoto, 19; Serhii Sobolevskyi/iStockphoto, 20

ISBN Information
9781503869738 (Reinforced Library Binding)
9781503881006 (Portable Document Format)
9781503882317 (Online Multi-user eBook)
9781503883628 (Electronic Publication)

LCCN 2022951394

Printed in the United States of America

ABOUT THE AUTHOR

Clara MacCarald is a freelance writer with a master's degree in ecology and natural resources. She lives with her family in an off-grid house nestled in the forests of central New York. When not parenting her daughter, she spends her time writing nonfiction books for kids.

CONTENTS

CHAPTER ONE

A WILD STRIKE

Ava and her aunt wade into the water carrying long fishing rods. A breeze rustles the trees around the creek. Ava and her aunt are **anglers**. This creek is their favorite fly fishing spot.

Ava aims her rod toward the deepest spot in the water, where fish might be feeding. She prepares to cast. Casting is how anglers use fishing rods to pitch their lures out onto the water. Lures are a type of fake fishing bait. Anglers can make lures move in different ways to attract fish.

Ava pulls out a long bit of fishing line from the rod. With one hand on the bottom of the rod, she carefully sweeps the tip above and behind her. A loop of line shoots backward. Then Ava casts the rod forward. The line soars over the water. At the end of the line is a fuzzy lure called a fly. The fly settles on the water's surface. Fish will think the fly is a tasty snack.

The United States has many rivers, lakes, and streams where people can go fly fishing.

Anglers must be gentle when handling the fish they catch. They should avoid squeezing the fish, touching its gills, or touching the fish with dry hands.

Ava watches the fly drift along, keeping one hand on the reel. The reel is a device attached to a fishing rod. It helps an angler wind in the line. Suddenly, a ripple appears in the water as a trout grabs the lure. Ava has a strike! She raises the rod, tugging the line so the fly hooks into the trout's mouth.

The fish fights as Ava pulls it in. Her aunt cheers her on. The trout jerks through the water until Ava gets it close. She dips her net in the water and guides the fish inside. Then she carefully pulls the hook out of the fish's lip.

Ava and her aunt aren't fishing for food today. They plan to let the fish go. This is called catch and release. The fish will be available to catch another day. It might also reproduce, increasing the trout population.

Ava wants a picture, but she doesn't want to harm the fish by keeping it in the air too long. She crouches down and lifts up the trout. Her aunt snaps a picture. Then Ava returns the fish to the water.

Fly fishing is a popular method of catching fish. It involves using a long fishing rod, heavy line, and a fly. People began fly fishing almost 2,000 years ago in Macedonia. This region is located north of Greece in southeastern Europe. Europeans practiced fly fishing hundreds of years ago. By the 1700s, European settlers brought fly fishing to North America. Today people fly fish in streams, rivers, lakes, and oceans.

CHAPTER TWO

FLY FISHING BASICS

Fly fishing requires a rod, reel, line, and lure. Fly rods are long, measuring 7 to 11 feet (2.1 to 3.3 m). They are often made of **fiberglass** or bamboo. Fly lines are made from different kinds of plastic, such as nylon. They are heavy. In regular fishing, the lure is heavy and the line is light. In fly fishing, it's the opposite. The lure is light and the line is heavy.

Anglers fly fish in water or from boats. Anglers in water stay dry by wearing wading boots and waders, or waterproof pants. Sometimes anglers wear vests with lots of pockets to carry supplies.

Fly rods are designed to be strong and flexible so they can bend without snapping. Fly rods come in three levels of flexibility: slow action, medium action, and fast action.

Some anglers buy special fly fishing vests with pockets and padding for warmth. These vests keep an angler's gear organized and protected while he fishes.

Anglers can catch many kinds of fish while fly fishing, including trout, salmon, crappies, yellow perch, and bluegills. Anglers can choose different sizes of gear depending on the size of fish they want to catch. To catch heavier fish, anglers must use heavier rods and lines.

Some anglers carry fly boxes packed with different kinds of flies. An angler watches the water's surface for insects. Then she chooses a fly that resembles the insects she finds.

When casting, anglers aim for areas where fish might be. Fish often gather near weeds or rocks, making ripples in the water as they feed. Anglers use different methods for casting, depending on the location and wind.

HATCHES

Insects such as mayflies lay eggs underwater. After hatching, young insects live below the surface. At certain times of year, hundreds of one kind of insect fly out of the water. Anglers call this a hatch. One famous hatch is the Hendrickson hatch. This mayfly's range is in the eastern and midwestern United States. The Hendrickson hatch is the first big hatch of the spring. Fish flock to the water's surface to eat the mayflies. Anglers who fish during this time use lures that look like mayflies to attract the fish. This makes fish more likely to strike anglers' lures.

Some anglers have large collections of flies. Fly boxes make it easy for anglers to organize and transport their flies. This helps anglers locate specific flies they want to use.

When a fish strikes, the angler pulls the line to catch the hook in the fish's mouth. He can pull the fish in by hand or by turning the reel. Then he guides the fish into a net.

There are many types of fly patterns. Each one resembles a different creature and can be used to attract different fish.

CHAPTER THREE

Fly Fishing Methods

There are three basic methods of fly fishing. The classic method is called dry fishing. It involves letting the fly drift on the water's surface. Anglers can see fish strike their lures.

In wet fishing, the fly sinks below the surface. Anglers might use flies that resemble insects or worms. Some anglers add a **bobber** to the line. The bobber floats until a fish grabs the lure. When the bobber disappears, the angler knows a fish is there.

In streamer fishing, anglers use streamer flies. These are bigger than other flies and often look like mice or fish. The angler moves the fly through the water. The quick movement excites fish and makes them bite the lure.

Anglers can use a variety of casting methods while fly fishing. Some common casting techniques are called the roll cast, the steeple cast, and the tuck cast.

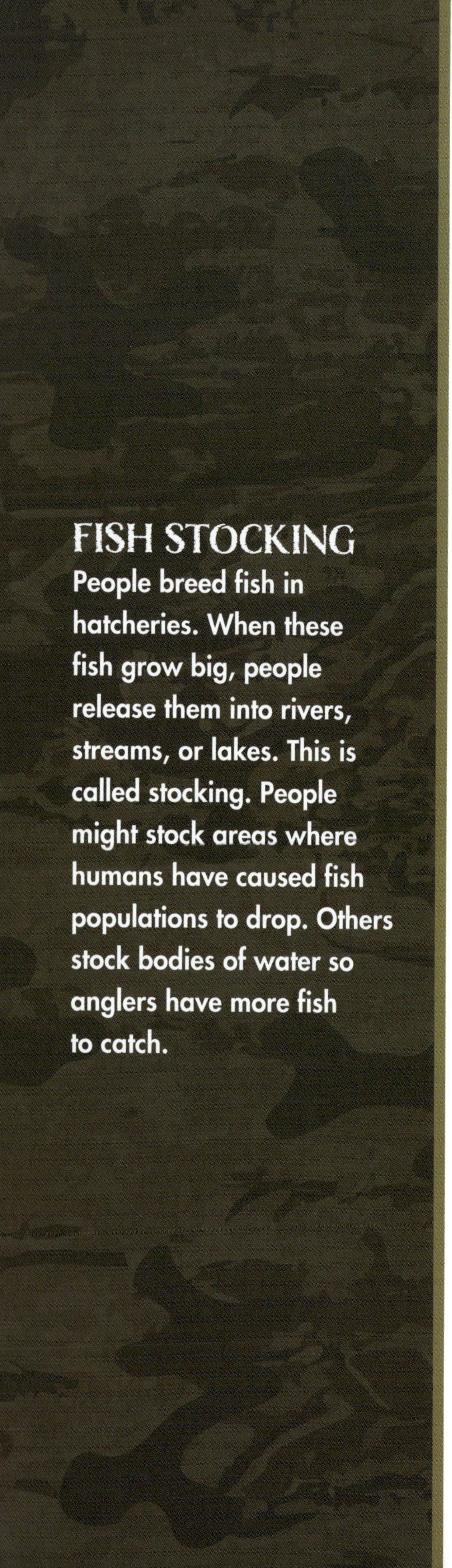

FISH STOCKING

People breed fish in hatcheries. When these fish grow big, people release them into rivers, streams, or lakes. This is called stocking. People might stock areas where humans have caused fish populations to drop. Others stock bodies of water so anglers have more fish to catch.

People fly fish in both salt water and fresh water. The big difference is that some saltwater fish, such as tarpon and sailfish, are much larger than freshwater fish. Catching these fish requires heavy gear made of materials such as stainless steel. It is also windy at sea, which makes casting harder.

Some anglers purchase lures from outdoor sports stores. Others make their own flies using feathers, fur, and yarn. They might create flies with wings, tails, or foam bodies that float.

To make a lure, an angler uses a **vise** to hold a hook. He ties thread onto the hook and then ties on the other parts of the fly. Anglers can learn many tricks for making different flies.

Some anglers eat the fish they catch. To prepare a fish, people remove its scales, guts, and head. Then they fry, bake, broil, or grill the fish.

Other anglers might choose to display their catches as **trophies**.

Some anglers go saltwater fly fishing on boats out at sea. Others fly fish in shallow ocean waters, where they can find fish such as bonefish.

Taxidermists can make models or statues from fish skin. An angler measures and photographs the fish. Then the taxidermist uses this information to make a trophy model.

CHAPTER FOUR

GETTING STARTED

To get started with fly fishing, anglers need the basic gear. They can buy or rent gear from outdoor sports stores. They may also be able to borrow gear from other anglers.

Beginners can practice casting on land or in the water. It can be helpful to practice with an experienced adult. Anglers should be careful when handling fishing hooks, which can catch on loose clothing and injure other anglers. As their lines move around, anglers should make sure the hooks don't come near anyone's skin. They should avoid wearing loose clothing, too. People should never fly fish alone in case of accidents or emergencies. Anglers wading alone in a creek could slip, hit their heads, and drown.

Anglers should also practice good **sportsmanship**. Responsible anglers follow all fishing rules in their region. They may need to purchase a fishing license. In the United States, money from fishing licenses supports **conservation**.

Some anglers fly fish from drift boats, letting wind and water move the boat as they fish. Anglers using drift boats should avoid disrupting other anglers and pay attention to changes in wind and weather.

Sometimes anglers must help a fish regain energy before releasing it. They should hold the fish in the water and gently move it back and forth. This helps water move through the fish's gills.

In many areas, human activity has changed bodies of water. People build docks and buildings near shores and pollute the water. This hurts fish populations. Conservation helps protect fish in these areas.

Other rules limit how, when, and where anglers can catch and keep specific fish. In 2022, anglers in New York could keep only three lake trout a day. Each trout had to be more than 21 inches (53 cm) long. These rules help keep fish populations stable and healthy. Different fishing spots may have different rules. For example, some areas ban hooks with a **barb**.

To find a fishing spot, beginners can ask adults in their families or at outdoor sports stores. Anglers can also go on guided fishing trips. A guide takes anglers to a fishing spot and teaches them new techniques. Some anglers attend fishing derbies, too. These are public fishing events where beginners can meet experienced anglers.

If an angler can't keep a fish, she should let it go. Catch and release is a good way to practice sportsmanship. A good sportsperson acts responsibly so future anglers can continue to enjoy fly fishing. Leaving fish in the water protects fish populations. It allows smaller fish to grow larger and reproduce.

An angler should also handle fish gently during catch and release. He can use a hook without a barb to protect the fish's mouth. He should reel in the fish quickly so it doesn't exhaust itself by fighting. He should keep it in the water as much as possible, too. He should let the fish go as soon as he can. By fly fishing responsibly today, anglers help make sure people can fly fish responsibly tomorrow.

GLOSSARY

anglers (ANG-lurz) Anglers are people who fish with a rod and line. The anglers went fly fishing at the creek.

barb (BARB) A barb is a sharp point on a hook that juts out and back. The barb on the end of a fishing line can catch on a fish's mouth.

bobber (BAH-bur) A bobber is a small floating object placed on a fishing line. When a fish strikes, the bobber dips underwater.

conservation (kon-sur-VAY-shuhn) Conservation is the protection of wildlife and other natural resources. Money from fishing licenses supports fish conservation.

fiberglass (FYE-bur-glas) Fiberglass is a strong material made from very thin glass fibers. People can make fly fishing rods out of fiberglass.

sportsmanship (SPORTS-muhn-ship) To have good sportsmanship means to act in a fair and reasonable way. Anglers can show good sportsmanship by not taking more fish from the water than they need.

taxidermists (TAK-sih-derm-ists) Taxidermists are people who prepare and mount animal skins to make realistic models. Anglers can take their catches to taxidermists.

trophies (TROH-feez) Trophies are things that are gained and displayed as a reminder of victory. Anglers can display fish as trophies of a successful fishing trip.

vise (VYSS) A vise is a device that holds an object in place. When making a fly, an angler uses a vise to hold the hook.

FAST FACTS

- Fly fishing is a method of fishing. It involves using a heavy line and a light lure called a fly. People can fly fish in rivers, streams, lakes, and oceans.
- A fly consists of a hook with other materials wrapped around it, such as thread and feathers. Flies often resemble insects or other creatures that fish eat.
- There are three basic fly fishing methods. These are called dry fishing, wet fishing, and streamer fishing.
- People can catch many types of fish when fly fishing. Common catches include bass, trout, salmon, and yellow perch.
- Anglers can practice good sportsmanship by following all safety guidelines and fishing rules in their area.

ONE STRIDE FURTHER

- How is fly fishing different from other kinds of fishing you know about? How is it similar?
- There are three methods of fly fishing. Why might an angler choose one type of fly fishing over the others?
- What are some ways to practice good sportsmanship while fly fishing? Why do you think it's important to practice good sportsmanship in the outdoors?

FIND OUT MORE

IN THE LIBRARY

Befus, Tyler. *The Orvis Kids' Guide to Beginning Fly Fishing: Easy Tips for the Youngest Anglers*. New York, NY: Skyhorse Publishing, 2021.

Kingston, Seth. *Fishing*. New York, NY: PowerKids Press, 2022.

Mazzarella, Kerri. *Fly Fishing*. New York, NY: Crabtree Publishing, 2023.

ON THE WEB

Visit our website for links about fly fishing:
childsworld.com/links

Note to Parents, Caregivers, Teachers, and Librarians: We routinely verify our Web links to make sure they are safe and active sites. So encourage your readers to check them out!

INDEX